RAINFOREST
HABITATS

Written by
Alex Hall

Rainforest © 2024 BookLife Publishing
This edition is published by arrangement with BookLife Publishing

sales@northstareditions.com
888-417-0195

Library of Congress Control Number:
2025930403

ISBN
979-8-89359-321-1 (library bound)
979-8-89359-405-8 (paperback)
979-8-89359-378-5 (epub)
979-8-89359-351-8 (hosted ebook)

Printed in the United States of America
Mankato, MN
092025

Written by:
Alex Hall

Edited by:
Noah Leatherland

Designed by:
Jasmine Pointer

American adaptation copyright © 2026 by North Star Editions, Mendota Heights, MN 55120. All rights reserved. No part of this book may be reproduced or utilized in any form or by any means without written permission from the publisher.

All facts, statistics, web addresses and URLs in this book were verified as valid and accurate at time of writing. No responsibility for any changes to external websites or references can be accepted by either the author or publisher.

Image Credits

All images are courtesy of Shutterstock.com. With thanks to Getty Images, Thinkstock Photo and iStockphoto.

Cover – Designsells, Maquiladora, Zhenyakot. Throughout – Vector Tradition, Overearth, hana honoka, Designsells, Maquiladora, Zhenyako. 4–5 – Curioso.Photography, Ondrej Prosicky, Harry Beugelink, Sergey Uryadnikov. 6–7 – Nily.eps, Maarten Zeehandelaar. 8–9 – Lukas Kovarik, Salparadis, Ondrej Prosicky, Flow 37. 10–11 – BlueRingMedia. 12–13 – Ronnie Howard, Sergey Uryadnikov, robuart. 14–15 – Yongkiet Jitwattanatam, yakub88. 16–17 – spatuletail, Anton_Ivanov. 18–19 – Uwe Bergwitz, VCoscaron. 20–21 – PARALAXIS, Stokkete, intararit. 22–23 – Dr Morley Read, soft_light.

CONTENTS

Page 4   Habitats Around the World
Page 6   Rainforest Climate
Page 8   Wildlife
Page 10   Layers of a Rainforest
Page 12   Jaguars
Page 14   Macaws
Page 16   Howler Monkeys
Page 18   Life Cycles
Page 20   Protect the Rainforests
Page 22   Our Rainforest Journey
Page 24   Glossary and Index

Words that look like this can be found in the glossary on page 24.

HABITATS AROUND THE WORLD

I'm an animal expert who explores habitats around the world. A habitat is the home where animals, plants, and other living things live. Are you ready to explore different habitats around the world?

Rainforest habitats are large areas with lots of trees and plants. These plants give food and shelter to the animals living there. The largest rainforest in the world is called the Amazon rainforest.

Amazon rainforest

RAINFOREST CLIMATE

Climate is the usual weather that happens in a place. It rains a lot in rainforests. The warm air there helps create more rainfall.

WILDLIFE

Rainforest habitats are home to half of the world's plant and animal species. These living things have <u>adapted</u> to life there.

Sloths have long claws for climbing trees. Sloths climb trees to stay away from <u>predators</u>.

8

LAYERS OF A RAINFOREST

The trees and plants create layers in a rainforest. The top layer is called the emergent layer. The layer below is the canopy. This is a thick layer of leaves and branches.

Emergent layer

Canopy layer

Many animals live in the canopy.

The next layer is the understory. This is where most shrubs and bushes grow. The bottom layer is the forest floor. This part of the rainforest is very dark and damp.

JAGUARS

Jaguars can be found on the forest floor in the Amazon. They have large paws. They also have strong <u>muscles</u>. They can climb trees. Jaguars are good swimmers. They often live near water.

Jaguars hunt at night. Their spotted fur helps them hide. They have very strong jaws to help them eat their prey.

We should keep our distance!

MACAWS

Macaws are colorful parrots. Many macaws live in the canopy of the Amazon. They have small bodies and tails. They can easily fly through gaps in the trees.

Macaws have sharp beaks. They can crack open nuts and seeds. Their beaks also help them climb up trees. They search for more food higher in the canopy.

They are better climbers than me!

HOWLER MONKEYS

Howler monkeys are <u>mammals</u>. Their long tails act as an extra arm. It allows them to grip onto branches. These monkeys mostly stay in the canopy.

Tail

Howler monkeys get their name from the sounds they make. They howl through the trees to mark their <u>territory</u>. Their howls can be heard up to 3 miles (5 km) away.

LIFE CYCLES

Life cycles are the different stages a living thing goes through.

One life cycle stage is to have young. Macaws have young by laying eggs. They make their nests inside dead trees.

18

After about a month, baby macaws <u>hatch</u>. The babies are born blind and featherless. Their feathers begin to grow about one week later. It takes about a month for the babies to be able to see.

They will be as colorful as their parents soon.

Baby macaws are called fledglings.

PROTECT THE RAINFORESTS

People are damaging rainforest habitats through deforestation. Trees are cut down and removed. Farms are often built in their place.

Many animals have lost their homes because of deforestation.

The rainforests need our help! You can help protect rainforests by buying food that is grown <u>sustainably</u>. You can also <u>recycle</u> paper so fewer trees are cut down.

OUR RAINFOREST JOURNEY

Wow! So many living things call rainforests home. There is still so much more to learn about these wonderfully wet and warm places.

GLOSSARY

adapted	changed over time to improve the chances of survival
equator	the imaginary line around the middle of the Earth
hatch	when a baby animal comes out of its egg
mammals	animals that are warm blooded, have a backbone, and produce milk to feed their children
muscles	the parts of the body that move the body around
predators	animals that hunt other animals for food
recycle	use something again to make something else
sustainably	in a way that uses products or energy without harming the environment
territory	an area claimed and defended by animals
toxins	harmful things made by plants or animals

INDEX

Amazon 5, 12, 14
eggs 18–19
Equator, the 7
feathers 9, 19
jaws 13
paws 12
rain 6–7
sun 7
tails 14, 16